fashion
illustration

basic

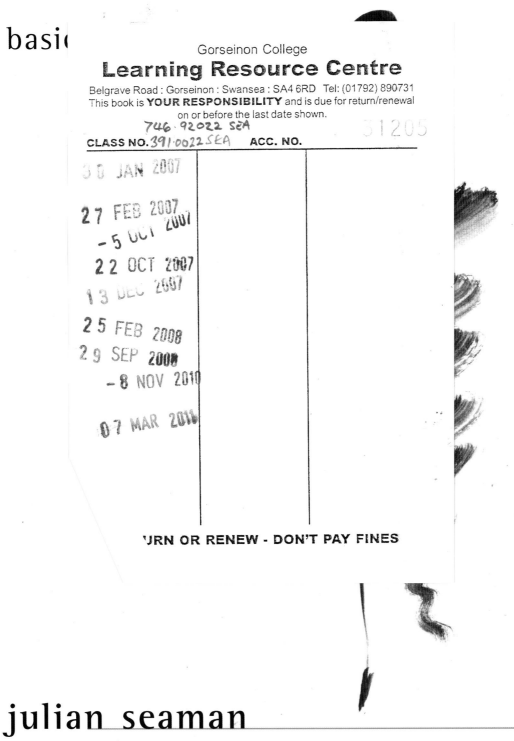

julian seaman

BT Batsford Ltd, London

5.99

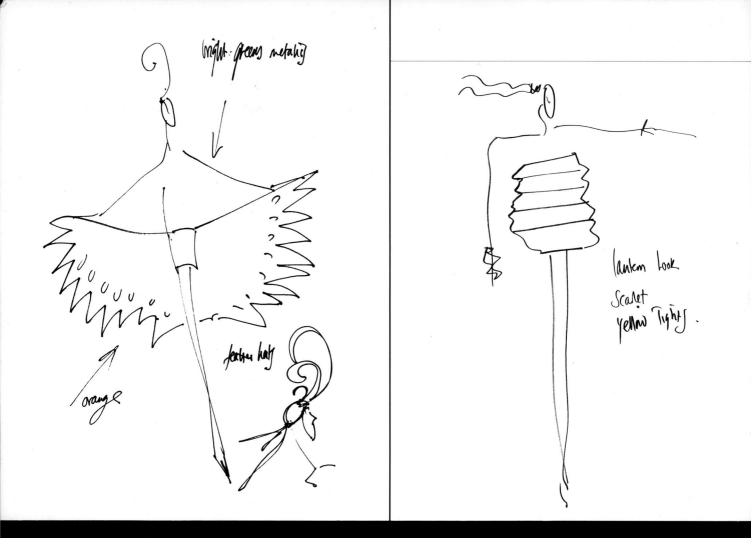

contents

foreword

I can never understand why so many people think that fashion designers get their inspiration floating in a midday bath, sipping a flute of champagne, or better still, lying on a glorious sun-soaked beach at St Tropez.

I've always thought in fashion there was only one quick way to success, and that course of action is not for the moral majority. Behind every stunning picture lies a lot of hard work, blood, sweat and raw nerves.

But now, Julian Seaman has made fashion illustration easier. He gives you the key to masses of clever ideas - and successful ones at that! And most importantly, there are simple, straightforward practical guides on how to achieve the different effects. After all, ideas don't make money, that's to be achieved in the execution of those ideas. With this book, inspiration should always be close at hand. This doesn't mean you shouldn't always be creating your own personal and individual style - but for ideas, this book is a boon. What a simple, clever idea of Julian's. Now why didn't I have an idea like that? Oh! Well! It's back to the beach and the sun for me again, I guess - or shall I try the bath today?

Enjoy your illustrating.

David Shilling

4

introduction

Creativity should be given the greatest possible

freedom, but this freedom needs to be harnessed

to an accessible form otherwise creation can

become just an esoteric exercise.

In the visual arts, experimentation in style

and media, along with a careful study of earlier

work, can create some of the best and most

original new designs and illustrations.

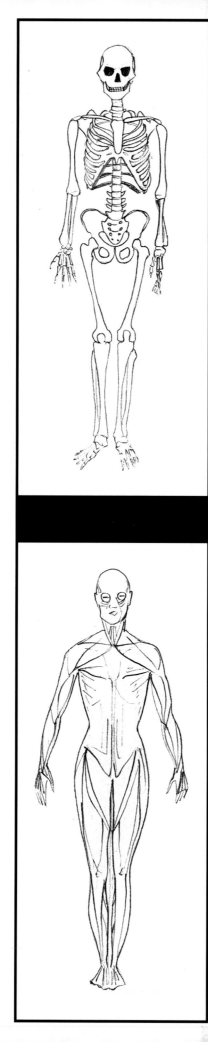

Fashion illustration differs from any other type of illustration only because of its subject matter. *Professional Fashion Illustration* (Batsford) explains many applications of this kind of art.

Fashion Illustration: Basic Techniques explores approaches and styles in a great variety of media, from pencil sketches to oil paintings.

Although an artist may eventually evolve a single personal style, continual experimentation helps to keep ideas fresh. Eyes should always be kept open for inspiration.

To make any intelligible statement, a creative person has to be in control of his or her tools: an articulate concept professionally presented.

The drawings on these first pages reiterate the lessons of *Fashion Drawing: The Basic Principles* (Batsford). Clothes cover people, skin covers muscle and muscle covers bones. It is always relevant to keep this in mind when indulging in more expressive pictures.

With so many different commercial applications, some illustrating materials are better than others for specific tasks - a sketch of a fashion show made as an *aide mémoire* will require totally different thinking to a full-blown colour finished drawing. Show sketches are included on the title pages.

The examples in this book are to encourage the aspiring illustrator to try out as many approaches as possible.

As an illustrator, I tend naturally towards bold, brightly-coloured drawings, but the constraints of monochrome pushed me in unknown directions. *Limitation* can spark *inspiration*.

The main part of *Fashion Illustration: Basic Techniques* shows what can be achieved when using a selection of readily-available artist's materials.

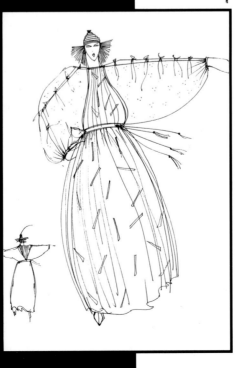

7

A short section on techniques for drawing

various textures and fashion fabrics follows,

and finally, there are examples of how to use

the styles of well-known artists for fashion

illustration.

Coloured crayons give a light feel to an illustration, so dense colour must be built up with overdrawing. This illustration shows an interesting mix of cultures with Arab racehorse owners in British traditional morning suits at Royal Ascot.

crayon
and
pencil

JULIAN SEAMAN 94

11

Although pencils come in various degrees of hardness, these two very different pictures were drawn with the same HB pencil, showing both a fully-realized illustration and a loose sketch approach.

Black felt tips are probably
the most used medium for
quick design sketches but they
are also employed for finished
artwork. They are available in
a large range of widths and
also in italic form.

14

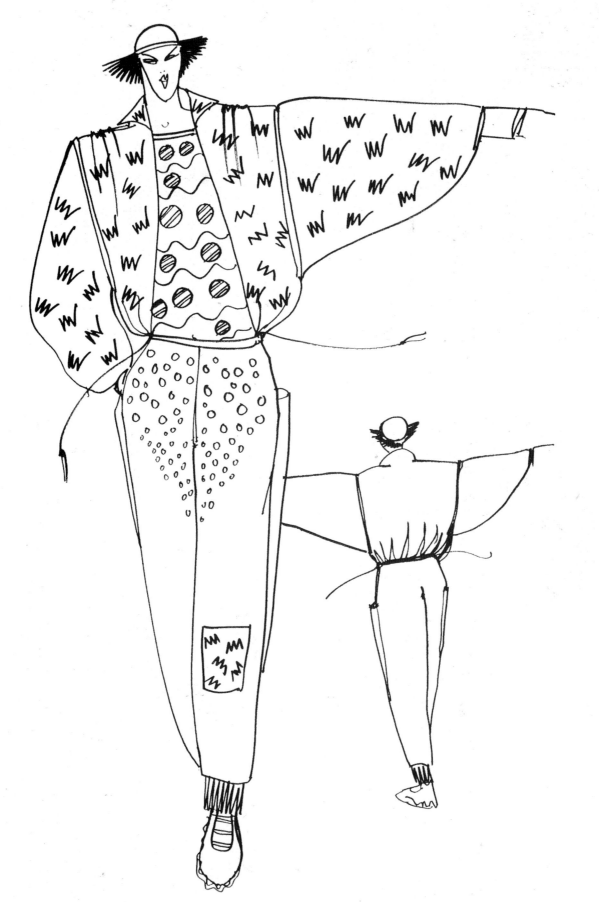

15

The 'magic' properties of the
felt tips have been used here to
produce a tartan effect.

16

wax crayon

Strong colours and a broad stroke freedom are the main
advantages of wax crayons. They are often quite soft,
so deliberate smudging can produce the effect of paint.
Wax crayons are not suitable for pinpoint detail, since
they never retain sharpness for more than a stroke.

18

A coloured background, whether

black or shaded in pastel,

can give a drawing immediate

strength since the first mark

will be a positive gesture.

20

An illustrator need not hold back from brave decisions - a ripped

surrounding can give a picture edge.

gouache

Gouache is perhaps the most widely used form of paint. Available in tubes, pots or powder, gouache can be employed as strong flat colour or thinly as a watercolour wash.

23

ballpoint pen

26

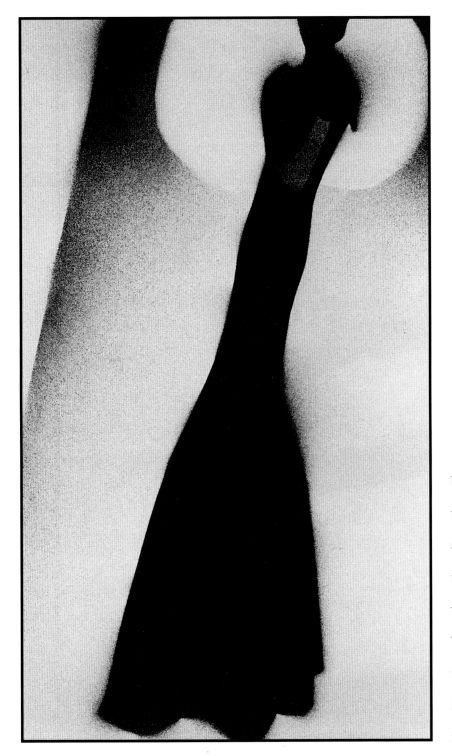

Based on a Man Ray photograph, this image was achieved by cutting out paper masks and spraying them from various distances.

The airbrush technique is ideal for creating soft transitions of shade and can be used with remarkable accuracy.

airbrush

Here, a portrait on canvas includes oil paint, wax crayon and
coloured ink. Not all media are compatible, but experimenting can
achieve unexpected results.

montage
and
collage

With montage and collage, designers can try all sorts of colour ways before committing themselves to the glue. A very thin pencil sketch on the backing paper will place the colour blocks accurately.

Ripped coloured paper gives clean flat colours which can show a fashion mood to good effect.

Ripped pieces of newspaper can be stuck down to make a picture.

Crosswords, bar codes and the darker parts of advertisements

are all useful.

This representation of a 1920s film star involved cutting the

'positive' image from white paper and sticking it to a black

background. The cutting process gives a unique feel - just a little

different from a photograph or a painting.

Collage can create a surreal
effect. Bits can be added on
from anywhere.

32

wax
and
wash

Wax crayons are water resistant, allowing the illustrator freedom to 'wash' background colours over the predrawn print designs. This technique contrasts the rigidity of the design with the freshness and translucence of the wash.

A household candle can be the

tool to note a pose.

34

Carefully aimed flicks from a scratchy fountain pen can give a drawing immediacy and vibrance.

ink

The laces, eyes and stitches are painted with latex before the wash
is applied. The latex is then peeled off to reveal the main design
feature. The designer has to apply a negative to achieve a positive.

38

This picture was built up from layers of paint and latex resist. This
can be used for all types of effect.

mixed
media 2

Putting together sources from unlikely places in unlikely ways is a luxury allowed to designers. A collage and drawing can incorporate a visual trick, here the facial features consist of a photograph of real skiers.

40

letratone™ and pantone™

Adhesive or rub-on textures and flat colour can enhance a drawing.
These dots mock up the effect of an enlarged comic strip or
newsprint photograph. They are also useful for filling in areas of
consistent shade or colour.

Rub-on textures with felt tip
outlines can give a well-defined
style idea.

42

The usual way to use these
natural drawing materials is
black on white.

Using chalk on dark paper can produce a positive image where the artist's eye must work in reverse and create a negative.

scraper board

A negative to positive effect can be achieved with a scraper board. White plaster on card is covered with a thin layer of black ink, revealing the white underneath when the image is worked.

50

lino cut

With a lino cut, the image,

gouged with specialist tools,

must be made in reverse to the

eventual design. This medium is

good for bold, stylized

illustrations.

Even nursery techniques can be used to create quite sophisticated paintings. Here, the lips and glasses are potato prints, while the hands provide a chance to be artistically messy.

potato print

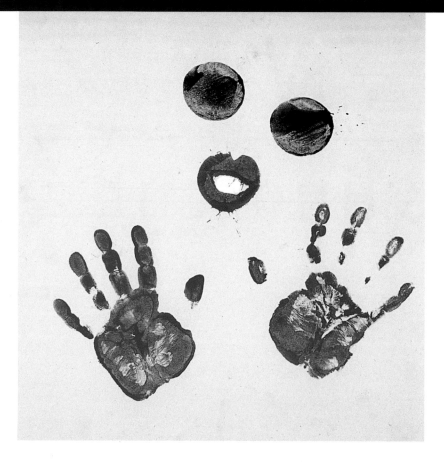

mixed
media3

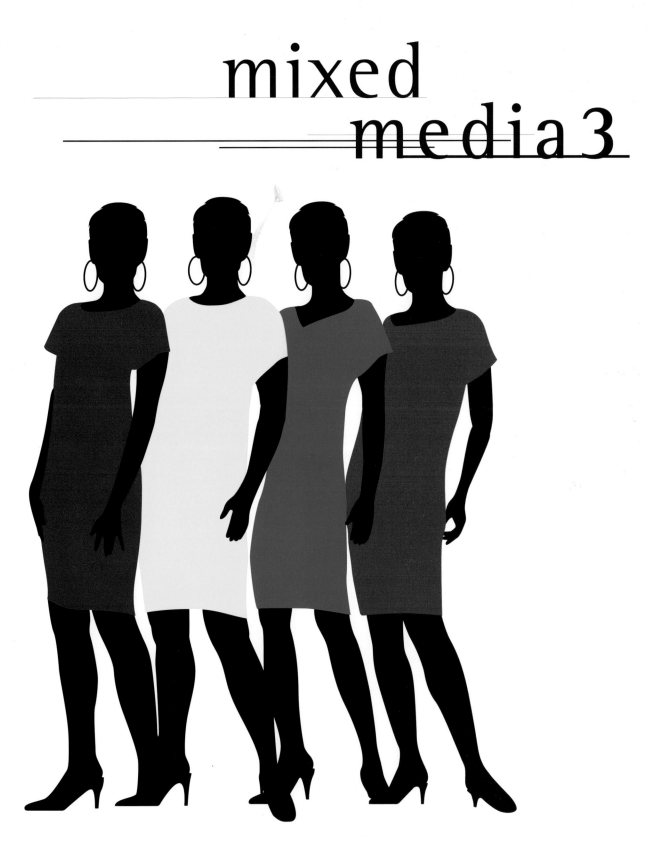

These silhouette figures have been originated from photographic

sources and rearranged, while the dresses are flat cut-outs from

coloured paper.

54

Dress print ideas can come from
many sources. A jungle look
was achieved by taking varying
photocopies and enlargements
from a single picture of
stampeding zebra, then cutting
them out and arranging them
into a garment shape.

A great image can always be

repeated in a different mediu

Gouache and ink replace

the photograph.

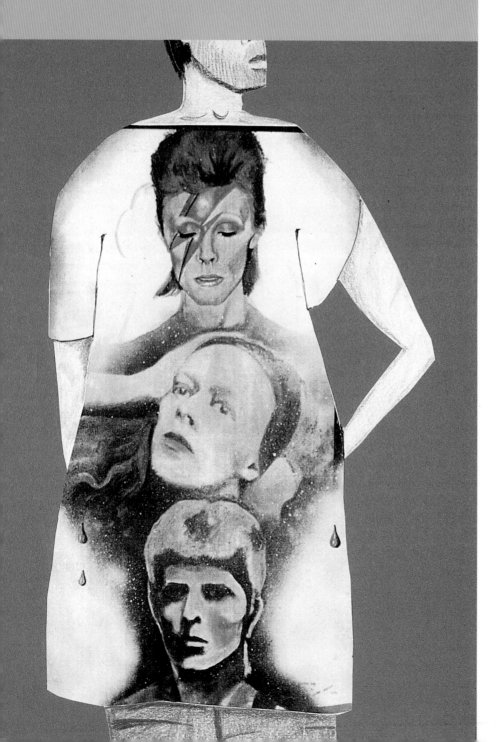

A retro T-shirt design has been developed from a photograph of an oil painting. The photocopy is cut out and stuck to coloured paper and the body drawn round the initial shape.

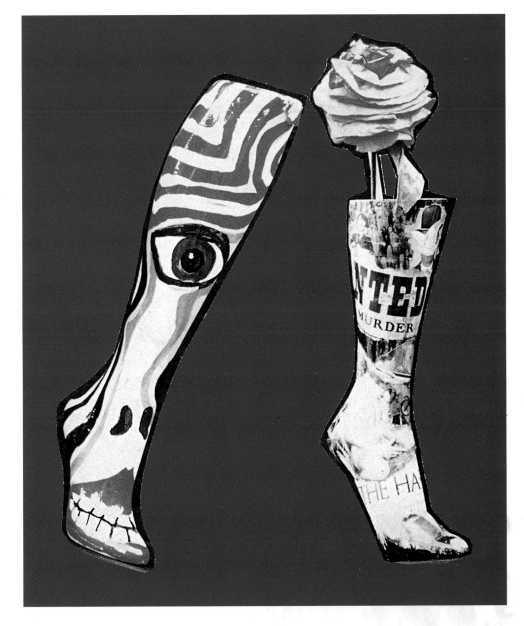

Fashion pictures do not just
show clothes, but also a
prevailing style. Found objects
can be painted or arranged in a
collage to create a feel.

58

All sorts of printed material can

work as a background. Old

phone books make a good

textured basis for a pastiche.

63

This simple drawing uses pencil

with felt tip.

64

Carefully-cut areas of transparent coloured Pantone™ adhesive film

have been applied to a black-and-white photocopy of a photograph

to give this Warhol-type image.

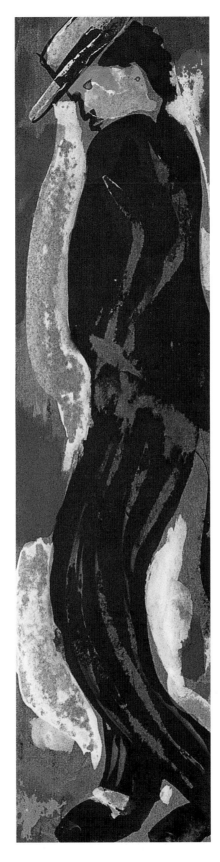

Here, a gouache painting was allowed to dry, then covered totally in black ink. It was then immediately run under a tap and carefully wiped down to give the marked effect to the background.

An alphabet supermodel.

fabrics

All clothing materials have a different feel, texture, structure and look. Certain types of paint, pen or crayon can illustrate a particular fabric more easily than others. The following pages show some examples.

leather

gouache

fur

watercolour on wet paper

fur

gouache on wrapping

and cut-out colour

paper background

70

velvet

cut-out shape in black paper with folds in soft pastel

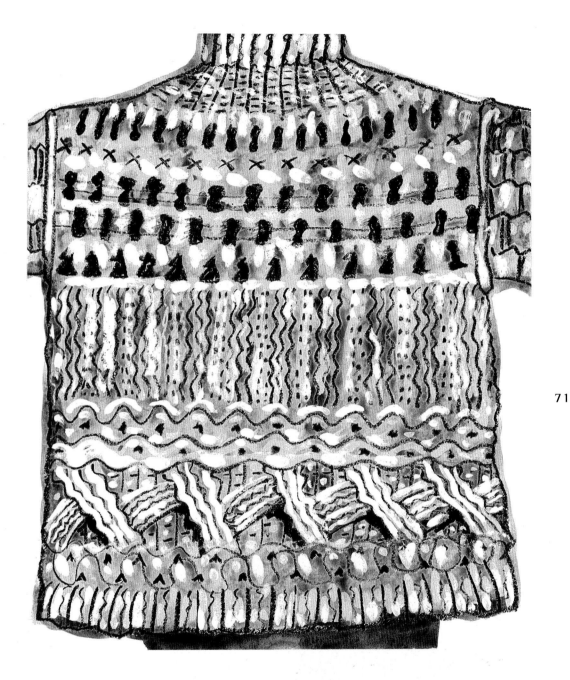

knit

wax resist and gouache

knit

pink pastels for the fluffy
angora feel, with the
harder edge of a felt tip
for the stockings

72

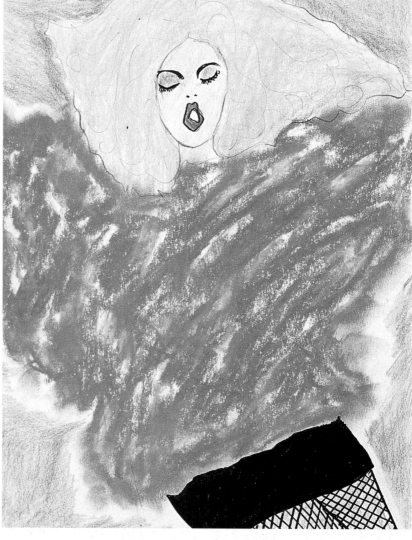

print

floral pattern rendered in latex

paint, watercolour wash before

the latex is peeled away

print

poster paint and pen and ink

74

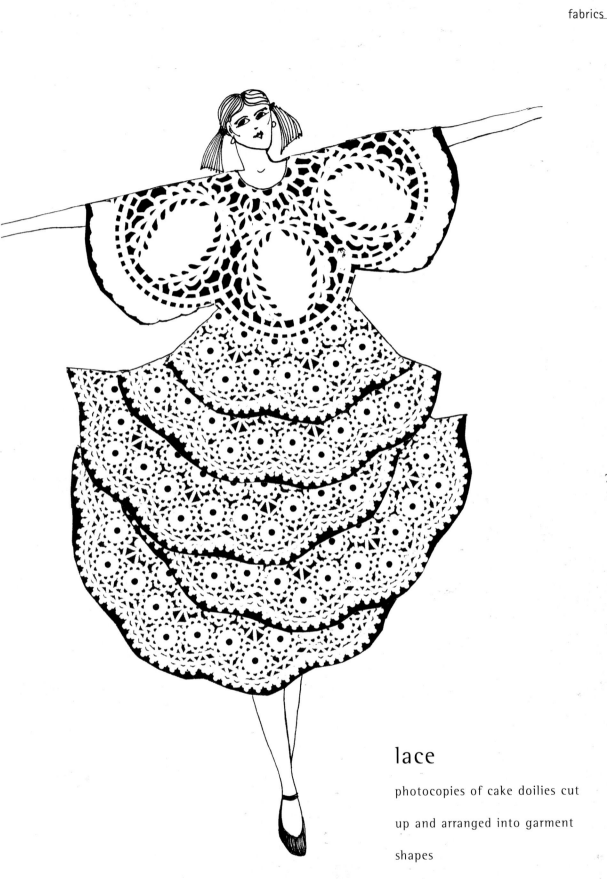

lace

photocopies of cake doilies cut

up and arranged into garment

shapes

76

make-up

real make-up - lipstick kiss,

mascara eyelashes,

blusher and eyeshadow

77

print

gouache, details with felt tip

and crayon

tweed

felt tip

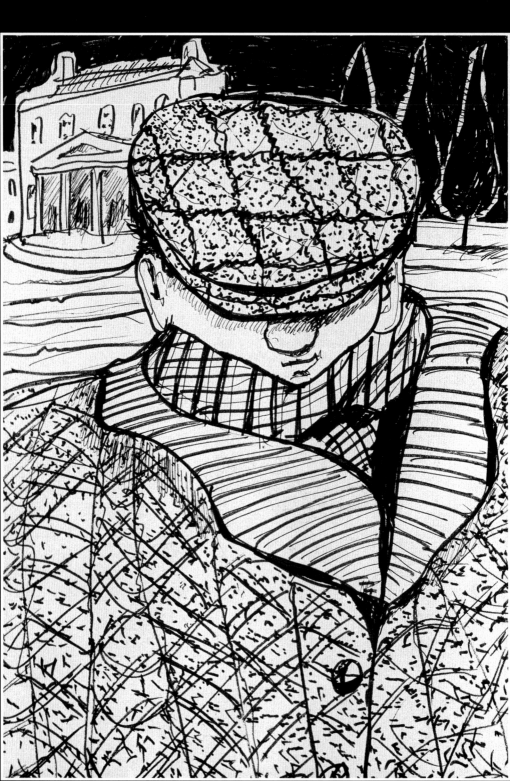

tartan

felt tip and pen

check

left to right:

crayon, felt tip, pastel, gouache

fine art references

81

Using recognizable fine art images can produce exciting modern designs. Experimenting with other artists' styles will greatly improve technique and help in the discovery of how various media work. Some sources for fashion drawing are established favourites, others can be more surprising. These pictures are just meant as a springboard for further experimentation.

after klimt

82

after tenniel

83

after famous five

after matisse

after lowry

86

after delaunay

87

after bridget riley

after picasso

after dufy

91

after escher

after beardsley

92

after lichtenstein

93

after toulouse-lautrec

94

after nineteenth-century japanese woodcut

Styles of illustration come in and out of fashion with almost the same regularity as clothes, but it is always useful to have points of reference so that an illustration will either reflect or project current trends. Where a writer must understand language, grammar and syntax, the visually creative person must hone artisan skills to express artistic intellect.

There are endless variations on any theme and new products to assist the artist continually arrive on the market. *Fashion Illustration: Basic Techniques* shows what one illustrator can do with a variety of techniques, materials and influences, and its aim is to encourage experimentation with new ideas.

conclusion